Photo by Carol Rosegg
Terri Klausner, Jason Workman, and Michael X. Martin in a scene from the Vineyard Theatre production of "Bed and Sofa." Set design by G. W. Mercier.

BED AND SOFA

A Silent Movie Opera

Music by
POLLY PEN

Libretto by
LAURENCE KLAVAN

Based on the Film by
ABRAM ROOM

DRAMATISTS
PLAY SERVICE
INC.

BED AND SOFA
Libretto Copyright © 1997, Laurence Klavan
Music Copyright © 1997, Polly Pen

ALL RIGHTS RESERVED

CAUTION: Professionals and amateurs are hereby warned that performance of BED AND SOFA is subject to a royalty. It is fully protected under the copyright laws of the United States of America, and of all countries covered by the International Copyright Union (including the Dominion of Canada and the rest of the British Commonwealth), and of all countries covered by the Pan-American Copyright Convention and the Universal Copyright Convention, the Berne Convention, and of all countries with which the United States has reciprocal copyright relations. All rights, including professional/amateur stage rights, motion picture, recitation, lecturing, public reading, radio broadcasting, television, video or sound recording, all other forms of mechanical or electronic reproduction, such as CD-ROM, CD-I, information storage and retrieval systems and photocopying, and the rights of translation into foreign languages, are strictly reserved. Particular emphasis is laid upon the matter of readings, permission for which must be secured from the Author's agent in writing.

The stage performance rights in BED AND SOFA (other than first class rights) are controlled exclusively by the DRAMATISTS PLAY SERVICE, INC., 440 Park Avenue South, New York, N.Y. 10016. No professional or non-professional performance of the Play (excluding first class professional performance) may be given without obtaining in advance the written permission of the DRAMATISTS PLAY SERVICE, INC., and paying the requisite fee.

Inquiries concerning all other rights should be addressed to Jack Tantleff, c/o The Tantleff Office, Inc., 375 Greenwich Street, Suite 700, New York, N.Y. 10013.

SPECIAL NOTE

Anyone receiving permission to produce BED AND SOFA is required (1) to give credit to the Author as sole and exclusive Author of the Play on the title page of all programs distributed in connection with performances of the Play and in all instances in which the title of the Play appears for purposes of advertising, publicizing or otherwise exploiting the Play and/or a production thereof. The name of the Author must appear on a separate line, in which no other name appears, immediately beneath the title and in size of type equal to 50% of the largest, most prominent letter used for the title of the Play. No person, firm or entity may receive credit larger or more prominent than that accorded the Author; and (2) to give the following acknowledgment on the title page of all programs distributed in connection with performances of the Play:

BED AND SOFA received its world premiere
at The Vineyard Theatre, New York City.

BED AND SOFA received its premiere at the Vineyard Theatre (Douglas Aibel, Artistic Director) in New York City, on February 1, 1996. It was directed by Andre Ernotte; the set and costume designs were by G. W. Mercier; the lighting design was by Phil Monat; music direction was by Alan Johnson; orchestrations were by John McKinney; the sound design was by Aural Fixation; and the production stage manager was Eileen Myers. The cast was as follows:

LUDMILLA	Terri Klausner
NIKOLAI (KOLYA)	Michael X. Martin
VOLODYA	Jason Workman

ON TAPE:
VOCALS	Polly Pen, Martin Moran
NARRATOR	Elizabeth Logun

BED AND SOFA was first produced as a workshop production at the Vineyard Theatre in June, 1995. The principal characters were the same except for VOLODYA who was played by Philip Lehl.

AUTHORS' NOTES

BED AND SOFA is based on a 1926 Russian silent film directed by Abram Room and written by Victor Shklovsky. The intention is to achieve the style of a silent movie, while avoiding melodrama or camp. The silent scenes should be played not as pantomime or parody but with each action and gesture as specific, clear, and strong as possible. Befitting the silent source material, the simplicity of the characters, and the "round robin" plot, the language is spare and ironically repeats; this is further highlighted by the changing musical settings.

PRODUCTION NOTES

To facilitate scene changes, the announcer's voice functions comically as an official "Soviet Realist" emissary; in New York, it was a dry "Ninotchka"-type female voice, coming from the radio. Also, in some scenes and during some changeovers, simple and essential sounds were used (a train, water dripping, kettle boiling, hammering, thunder, rain, cats fighting, pigeons mating, footsteps, a heartbeat).

A set could include a second level, which could effectively imply the roof of the Bolshoi Opera, where Nikolai works. The set could also feature a toy train. It would appear on a little track, with train sounds, three times: at the beginning; when Nikolai returns from his business trip; and at the end. If other productions feature a train, the following voice-over can be read in the scene change after the second checkers game, after Ludmilla has been stymied by the two men ignoring her, on script page 37.

> ANNOUNCER'S VOICE.
>   Perhaps this would be an excellent time for a very tiny
>   Anna Karenina to throw herself in front of that little train.

NOTE: This is an acting edition. Anyone producing this work must refer to the score for the complete lyrics. (Even though the lyrics are printed here in lower-case type, BED AND SOFA is through-sung.)

CAST OF CHARACTERS

LUDMILLA, dark, attractive, thirties. A beleaguered, complacent, dreamy Russian housewife.

NIKOLAI, "Kolya," hearty, energetic, dark-haired, thirties. A cheerful domestic despot.

VOLODYA, blonde, thirties, with a sensitive face. A political idealist.

BED AND SOFA

An anthem plays. Then:

ANNOUNCER'S VOICE.
>*Bed and Sofa* is a musical adaptation of a silent
>film made by Abram Room. It is set seventy years
>ago in the Soviet Union, when no one could say
>very much. My friends, remember, as Lenin wrote,
>"Liberty is precious. So precious that it must be rationed."

(Lights rise on a flexible set, suggesting inside and outside. Outside are impressions of Moscow in 1926: a train, a church, streets. Inside is a cramped middle-class flat: a bed, a table, a dressing screen. Two people, Ludmilla and Nikolai, lie asleep in the bed, dressed in period underclothes. The sound of a train. In the outside area, as if traveling, Volodya stands, excitedly. He is a blonde man in his thirties with a sensitive face. He wears a cap and coat and carries a simple bag. For a long time, he travels and the two sleep. Then:)

VOLODYA.
>The train! The train! The train!
>The birds! The morning! The sun!
>The bridge! The city! The sky!
>Outside! The world!

(In the apartment ... Nikolai [hereafter addressed as "Kolya"], is a hearty, energetic, dark-haired man in his thirties. Ludmilla, is dark, attractive, beleaguered. He teases her awake.)

LUDMILLA.
>The world. Inside.

NIKOLAI.
>A Stalin wall calendar.

LUDMILLA.
>November 3rd.

LUDMILLA and NIKOLAI.
>1926. Moscow. Russia.

LUDMILLA.
>The bed. The sofa.

NIKOLAI.
>The brush. The water. The wash.

LUDMILLA.
>   The dressing screen.

NIKOLAI.
>   The cat. The tea.

LUDMILLA and NIKOLAI.
>   The table. With two leaves.

LUDMILLA.
>   Inside it is quiet and dark.

NIKOLAI.
>   The stain.

LUDMILLA.
>   The drain.

LUDMILLA and NIKOLAI.
>   13 Meschanskaia Lane.

(At the same time:)

VOLODYA.
>   The train! The train! The train!

NIKOLAI.
>   The brush. The water. The wash.

LUDMILLA.
>   The cat. The tea.
>   The table. With two leaves.

VOLODYA.
>   The birds! The morning! The sun!

LUDMILLA.
>   The dressing screen.

VOLODYA.
>   The bridge! The city! The sky!
>   Outside, it is noisy and bright.

LUDMILLA.
>   Inside I dream.

LUDMILLA and NIKOLAI.
>   The bed. The sofa.
>   The world. Inside.

VOLODYA and NIKOLAI.
> Outside!

ALL.
> The world!
> 1926. Moscow. Russia.

(Volodya gets off the train. Ludmilla and Nikolai go through a very detailed morning ritual. He tears off a calendar page, balls it up and flicks it good-naturedly at her. She indulges him in this. She makes the bed. He goes offstage and showers. He comes back on, drying his hair with a towel. She goes off and scrambles eggs. Outside, Volodya studies a map of the city. Nikolai does some exercises.)

NIKOLAI. *(Spoken.)*
> Jump! Jump! Jump!

(Then Nikolai takes his place at the table. Ludmilla re-enters and serves him his eggs. He cannot eat them, they are too runny. She shrugs, goes to the door, makes kissing sounds, and leaves the plate outside for the cat. Then:)

VOLODYA. *(Sung.)*
> My name is Volodya! My name is Volodya!
> I have blonde hair and a sensitive face!

NIKOLAI.
> Nikolai. Stone mason and construction supervisor.

LUDMILLA.
> Ludmilla. His wife.
> The photograph of my face in a frame.

VOLODYA.
> Today I begin my job.
> As a printer for a paper.

NIKOLAI.
> My job is on the roof of the Bolshoi Opera.

LUDMILLA.
> My job ...

(Nikolai rises from the table, puts on his cap and coat. He turns to Ludmilla.)

NIKOLAI.
> Don't forget to scrub the floor.

(Smiling, he kisses her goodbye, ebulliently. Then he exits. Ludmilla waits alone for a minute. Then — resignedly:)

LUDMILLA.
> His majesty. The husband.

(Nikolai moves outside, into the city, heads for work. Inside, Ludmilla picks up her dust cloth, to start cleaning. She turns on the radio, which is broken, and only hisses static. Undeterred, she dances to the grating sounds. Then she sits, idly, combs her hair with her fingers. Outside, Volodya looks around at the city, while Nikolai — who has reached his workplace on the roof of the Bolshoi Opera — takes a break for lunch, eats a sandwich, and looks out at the city, satisfied.)

NIKOLAI.
>I have wrapped my sandwich in paper.
>I eat my sandwich on the statue of a horse.
>Looking down at the street —

VOLODYA.
>Looking up at the clouds,
>at the statues of horses —

LUDMILLA.
>Looking out of the window, at the train.
>I am cleaning.

NIKOLAI.
>I am eating.

VOLODYA.
>I am changing the world.

LUDMILLA.
>Looking out —

VOLODYA.
>Looking up —

NIKOLAI.
>Looking down —

VOLODYA.
>A printer! A paper! A job!

NIKOLAI.
>The lunch. The sandwich. The wrapper.

LUDMILLA.
>The window. The train.

VOLODYA.
>The future! A job!

NIKOLAI.
> Outside. I eat.

LUDMILLA.
> Inside. I dream.

VOLODYA.
> The future! A world!

LUDMILLA.
> The world. I dream.

NIKOLAI.
> I eat.

LUDMILLA.
> Inside. The home.

(Nikolai gets ready to leave work. Volodya takes an official-looking piece of paper from his pocket.)

NIKOLAI.
> I won't stay for the meeting ...

VOLODYA.
> The future!

NIKOLAI.
> I like it better at home.

(Volodya reads the official-looking piece of paper. Stunned:)

VOLODYA.
> News! I need a home.

NIKOLAI.
> I like it better at —

LUDMILLA and NIKOLAI.
> 13 Meschanskaia Lane.

ANNOUNCER'S VOICE.
> It may be difficult to imagine but, at this time,
> in a large city, apartments were hard to find and small.

VOLODYA.
> They say that
> Without a home, I can't get work.

Without my work,
I don't know what I'll do.
What will I do then?
I'm not like other men.

When I'm at work, I'm a man
Who never needs a meal,
Who never wants a woman.
I'm not aware of breathing
When I'm at work.

Without my work,
I'm drifting like a piece of paper
Blown into the homes of people.
Picked up and thrown away by people.
I'm never good with people.
I'm never good in homes.

It's more than just the money.
Without my work,
I don't know what I'll do.
What will I do then?
I'm not like other men, I'm alone.

I must get lodgings.
(Desperately — spoken:)

There is a housing shortage!

ALL.
Short.
Shor ...

Shh.
Stalin.
(Thunder and lighting. Sung:)

VOLODYA.
The world. Outside.

NIKOLAI.
Inside. The home.
(As Nikolai heads home, he and Volodya approach each other.)

VOLODYA.
The night. The cold. The rain.

12

NIKOLAI.
> The night. The cold. The rain.

(The two men bump into each other. They are shocked.)

VOLODYA.
> Kolya?

NIKOLAI.
> Volodya?

(They hug.)

VOLODYA and NIKOLAI.
> My friend! My friend!

VOLODYA.
> A printer! A paper!

VOLODYA and NIKOLAI.
> My friend! My friend!

(They hug again.)

NIKOLAI.
> Construction …

VOLODYA. *(Unimpressed.)*
> My friend.

NIKOLAI.
> Supervisor!

VOLODYA. *(Impressed.)*
> My friend!

VOLODYA and NIKOLAI.
> My friend!

(They hug again.)

NIKOLAI. *(Refers to apartment.)*
> Ludmilla!

VOLODYA.
> Ludmilla?

NIKOLAI.
> Ludmilla!

VOLODYA. *(Understands.)*
> His wife.

NIKOLAI.
    Inside ...

LUDMILLA.
    Inside. I dream.

ALL.
    Inside! Inside! The home!

VOLODYA and NIKOLAI.
    My friend!
(They hug a last time.)

BLACKOUT

In the apartment, her dust cloth swinging, Ludmilla is dancing exotically to the static. She turns and sees — Volodya standing there. She screams. Concerned, Volodya tries to calm her. He has his bag.

VOLODYA.
    My name is Volodya! My name is Volodya!
(Ludmilla calms. She considers him. To herself:)

LUDMILLA.
    He has blonde hair and a sensitive face.
(Nikolai has entered behind his friend. Heartily:)

NIKOLAI.
    Volodya! My friend!
(Relieved, Ludmilla catches her breath. She shakes his hand.)

LUDMILLA.
    Ludmilla. His wife.
    Would you ...
(Volodya and Nikolai explain:)

VOLODYA and NIKOLAI.
    We were in the war together.
    We marched. And sang.
    We drank. And we smoked cigarettes.
    And we maimed. And we killed.
    In the war together!
(They start to weep. Ludmilla thinks they are finished. Politely, she asks:)

LUDMILLA.
> Would you like ...

(But they are not finished:)

VOLODYA and NIKOLAI.
> We were in the war together.
> We froze. And starved.
> We bled. And we died.
> We were disemboweled.
> Then we decomposed.

LUDMILLA.
> Would you like ...

NIKOLAI.
> We were eaten by worms.

VOLODYA.
> We were eaten by worms.

VOLODYA and NIKOLAI.
> Which spread disease.
> Causing others to die.
> Then we came back to life —
> in the war together!

(Overcome by the memories, the two men kiss and embrace. Ludmilla sees they are finally finished. Politely, she asks:)

LUDMILLA.
> Would you like a ...

NIKOLAI.
> ... place to sleep.
> There is a housing shortage.

VOLODYA.
> Not a vacant room in Moscow.

(Ludmilla looks at Volodya. Then she speaks to both men. Her answer is positive.)

LUDMILLA.
> Not another word.

(Then:)
> We'll take the bed and you the sofa.

(Volodya and Nikolai are surprised. Then, looking at each other, they are exultant.)

NIKOLAI.
> The bed!

VOLODYA.
> The sofa!

NIKOLAI.
> The dressing screen!

VOLODYA.
> I'll take the sofa and you —

VOLODYA and NIKOLAI.
> The bed!
> The sofa!
> The dressing screen!

VOLODYA.
> A place to sleep!

NIKOLAI.
> Inside!

LUDMILLA.
> A place to sleep ...
(Ludmilla is looking at Volodya. To herself — interested:)
> He has blonde hair and a sensitive face.
(Then catching herself:)
> Not another word.
(Ludmilla begins making up the sofa. The two men begin setting up the dressing screen between the two areas. They clown around, convulsing themselves. Subsiding, they turn and see Ludmilla standing there, watching, uncomprehending. Then she turns and makes kissing noises for the cat. Lights fade.)

ANNOUNCER'S VOICE.
> Trotsky said, "It is imperative that every man and
> woman devote full attention to the order and
> cleanliness of the house. Otherwise, you end up
> with a foul, lice-ridden pit."
(Lights up. All are at work: Ludmilla is in the apartment, cleaning; Volodya is at his printing office; Nikolai is at his construction job, on the roof of the Bolshoi Opera.)

LUDMILLA.
> The stain.

VOLODYA.
> A printer.

LUDMILLA.
> The drain.

NIKOLAI.
> My job is on the roof of the Bolshoi Opera.

ALL.
> 13 Meschanskaia Lane.

(Ludmilla sits by the window, dreaming. Volodya finishes work. He leaves and approaches the apartment. From the window, Ludmilla watches him. Then she quickly moves from it and starts to primp a bit at the mirror, combing her hair with her fingers. Volodya is about to enter. Seeing him, Ludmilla feigns going back to her cleaning. Volodya enters. Ludmilla smiles at him, trying not to seem too happy to see him. He carries a bundle with him. He puts it down on the table. He unwraps it. He takes out ... a newspaper. He shows it to her.)

VOLODYA.
> A paper.

(Ludmilla cannot contain her excitement.)

LUDMILLA.
> A paper! News!

(He hands it to her. She sits and greedily reads. Then, she looks up from it, at him. Volodya smiles. Then, with even more drama, as if he is showing her a jewel, he takes out from his bundle something else:)
> A radio!

VOLODYA.
> That works!

LUDMILLA.
> The world!

LUDMILLA AND VOLODYA.
> News!

(Ludmilla stares at it, transfixed. Then she turns it on. We hear only static. Then, fuzzily:)

NEWSMAN.   *(Spoken.)*
> Over Radio Moscow
> The Red and the — White and the
> Comrade's Flag —
> March at a meeting
> Radio Moscow
> News —
> Over ...

(Ludmilla tunes it. Then, to her surprise, she hears:)

MALE SINGER.
> — the, over the moon!
> I'm in the sky up above!
> I'm flyin' high, 'coz I'm in love!
> You send me over the moon!

(The song escalates romantically. They are made uncomfortable.)

MALE and FEMALE SINGERS.
>You send me over the moon!
>I'm in the sky up above
>I'm flyin' high, 'coz I'm in love!
>You send me — uh, oh! — over the ...

(Just then, Nikolai bursts in, holding a telegram.)

NIKOLAI.
>News!

(They turn, as if caught with each other.)

LUDMILLA and VOLODYA.
>News!

NIKOLAI.
>A telegram! I'm being sent on a trip to the new housing project in Rostov!

ALL.
>A telegram! News!

(Ludmilla is rushing around, packing for Nikolai. He stands, impatiently, excitedly, near her.)

LUDMILLA and VOLODYA.
>When?

NIKOLAI.
>In twenty minutes.

ALL.
>The train! The train! The train!

NIKOLAI.
>In twenty minutes.
>For three weeks.

LUDMILLA and VOLODYA.
>He's being sent to Rostov!

ALL.
>The train! The train! The train!

NIKOLAI.
>In thirteen minutes.
>For three weeks.

ALL.
>   He's (I'm) being sent to Rostov!

(Volodya now stands. We see he, too, has been packing. Both Ludmilla and Nikolai are shocked.)

NIKOLAI.
>   Volodya!

VOLODYA.
>   I shouldn't stay here while you're away.
>   People will talk rubbish.

NIKOLAI.
>   Ludmilla is crazy about me.
>   She knows I'm fond of her.

LUDMILLA.
>   Rubbish! *(Then covers.)* The brush. The water.
>   The wash.

VOLODYA.
>   People will talk.

NIKOLAI.
>   She'll take the bed and you the sofa.

VOLODYA.
>   The train! The train!

LUDMILLA.
>   His majesty, the husband.

VOLODYA.
>   The train!

LUDMILLA.
>   Ludmilla, his wife.

NIKOLAI.
>   She knows I'm fond of her.

ALL.
>   The train! The train! The train!

NIKOLAI.
>   In seven minutes.
>   For three weeks.

(Ludmilla hands Nikolai his packed bag. He stands at the door. To Ludmilla, ebulliently:)
    And don't forget to scrub the floor!
(Ludmilla extends her cheek for a kiss. But jubilantly, he only exits. There is an uncomfortable pause between Ludmilla and Volodya, alone together in the apartment. Then:)

VOLODYA.
    You'll take the bed and I the sofa?

LUDMILLA.
    You'll take the sofa and I the bed.

VOLODYA.
    You'll take the bed and I the sofa.

LUDMILLA.
    You'll take the sofa and I the bed.
(They repeat, trading off parts of lines. Through this, excruciatingly, he crumples a pillow on the sofa, she rocks the rocking chair — ever faster — he hangs up his coat, she collapses on the bed, seems to swim from side to side.)

VOLODYA.
    You and I.

LUDMILLA.
    Bed and sofa?

VOLODYA.
    You and I.

LUDMILLA and VOLODYA.
    Sofa and bed.
(Then — each lurches stiffly across the room, towards each other.)

VOLODYA.
    You.

LUDMILLA.
    And.

VOLODYA.
    I. Bed.

LUDMILLA.
    And.

VOLODYA.
    Sofa.

LUDMILLA.
    You.

VOLODYA.
    And.

LUDMILLA.
    I. Sofa.

VOLODYA.
    And.

LUDMILLA.
    Bed.
(Until:)

LUDMILLA and VOLODYA.
    And ... the dressing screen!
(Gratefully, they set up the dressing screen between each other. Then both go into their respective corners: Ludmilla on the bed, Volodya on the sofa. They stay there, awake, for a long time. Lights fade.)

ANNOUNCER'S VOICE.
    Marx wrote, "Man is a sensuous being, and to be
    sensuous is to suffer."
(Lights up on the "outside" part of the set. Ludmilla and Volodya walk on the street.)

LUDMILLA.
    It's been such a long time since I
    last went to the movies.
    I seldom have the honor of going out
    with my husband.
(They reach a movie theater. They enter. Lights flicker. They stand and watch. Transfixed.)
    The screen! The world!
SOUND OF SOMEONE IN THE AUDIENCE.   Shh!
LUDMILLA.   Not another word.
(They politely sit. The silent movie plays. Ludmilla watches, entranced. Volodya watches her watch. Nostalgic, pastoral music.)
    She is beautiful.

VOLODYA.
    She is beautiful.
(Watching her, he wipes a tear falling from her cheek. Then — the tempo of the music accelerates: adventure.)

LUDMILLA and VOLODYA.
>So exciting.
>So exciting.

(*Both lean forward, nearly standing, with excitement.*)
>What will happen now?!

(*Both scream.*)
>Jump!

(*Then — a sigh of relief. They sit back. The music becomes comical. They start, slowly, to laugh, until they are nearly hysterical.*)

VOLODYA.
>Look — there's a little tramp
>With dancing bread.
>On a fork.

(*Music shifts again, slows, to tragedy. Soberly:*)

LUDMILLA.
>She is walking in a circle
>Growing smaller.
>She is going away
>With her child.

VOLODYA.
>Go back!

LUDMILLA.
>She is gone in the dark.
>The end.

(*The flickering ends. They are staring at the screen. Lights fade. Lights rise in the apartment. Ludmilla and Volodya enter after their night out. Volodya helps her off with her coat. Ludmilla goes to the mirror. She combs her hair with her fingers. Then:*)
>The mirror. A woman. My face.

(*Volodya has approached. He stands behind her. He puts his hands on her shoulders. Slowly, she pulls away. Then — Volodya takes out a pack of cards. He shows them to her. Ludmilla hesitates. Then she nods. He offers her one. She takes it. Slowly, she looks at the card. Then, seeing it — disturbed — it is:*)
>His majesty.

(*Upset, she starts to go. He stops her. He shows her his card.*)

VOLODYA.
>His wife.

(*He gently takes the card from her. With his own, he places them back into the deck together. They look at each other. Then, helplessly:*)

LUDMILLA.
>Fond of.

LUDMILLA and VOLODYA.
>Crazy about.
(They are closer. Then — suddenly, the whole deck slips out of his hands. They kneel, frantically, trying to retrieve the cards. Then, looking into each other's eyes, they freeze. Still staring at each other, they rise.)
>You and I.
>Bed or sofa?
>You and I.
>Sofa or bed?
>You and I.
>Bed or sofa?
>You and I.
>Sofa or bed?
>So exciting.
>Not another word.

(They kiss then. They move onto the sofa. Ludmilla whispers passionately to him.)

LUDMILLA.
>Volodya.

LUDMILLA and VOLODYA.
>Inside.

(They start to make love. The lights fade. Lights rise. Early morning. The two of them are on the sofa. Volodya sleeps. Ludmilla rises. She looks at him, fondly. She walks slowly away. She sees:)

LUDMILLA.
>A Stalin wall calendar. February 9th.

(She touches it, tenderly, as if to mark the date. She sees the deck of cards, still scattered on the floor. She kneels and retrieves them. Then she picks up one card.)
>Nine.

(She goes to sit upon the bed. There Ludmilla is troubled. She bites the top of the headboard. Then she rises and returns to the sofa. She sits beside Volodya. He stirs. He sees her, sleepily. He smiles. Then realization of what they have done grabs him also. He sits up, stunned. Reassuringly, she places her head on his shoulder. Lights fade on them.)

ANNOUNCER'S VOICE.
>Arriving early can be worse than being late ...
>especially if you are attending a dinner party or
>your wife is having an affair with your friend.

(Lights rise. Nikolai now appears, on a train, traveling home.)

NIKOLAI.
>The train. The train. The train.
>The birds. The morning. The sun.

(Volodya is at his job. Ludmilla is in the apartment, sewing. Their thoughts are drifting. With growing alarm:)

VOLODYA.
>Kolya. For three weeks.

LUDMILLA.
>Kolya. The stain. Inside. The bed.

VOLODYA.
>Kolya. What will Kolya say?

LUDMILLA.
>Kolya. The stain. Inside. The bed.

(Nikolai gets off the train. He begins approaching the apartment. At the same time:)

NIKOLAI.
>The lunch. The sandwich. The wrapper.

LUDMILLA and VOLODYA.
>Kolya. What will Kolya say?

NIKOLAI.
>The bridge. The city. The sky.

LUDMILLA.
>Volodya. I dream.

VOLODYA.
>Ludmilla. I dream.

LUDMILLA.
>February 9th.

NIKOLAI.
>Home! Home! Home!

(Behind Ludmilla, Nikolai enters the apartment. Ludmilla pricks her finger with the needle. She turns, sees him. Then:)

LUDMILLA.
>Kolya!

(Ludmilla stares at him.)
>What will happen now?

(Nikolai advances, threateningly. He is holding something behind his back. She retreats, afraid, sorry, shocked. She cowers, ready for the blast. Then ... he takes out ... a small box. It is a gift. Ludmilla looks at it and him stunned. Then — smiling — he opens it. Then:)

NIKOLAI.
>Beans!

LUDMILLA.
> Beans?

NIKOLAI.
> I have brought you beans! For coffee!
> Coffee beans! Coffee from Rostov!

LUDMILLA.
> Coffee —

NIKOLAI.
> Beans! I have brought you coffee beans!
> Coffee beans! From Rostov!

(Then, with infinite relief — understanding:)

LUDMILLA.
> You ... have ... brought ... me ... beans!

LUDMILLA and NIKOLAI.
> Beans! Beans! Coffee beans!
> Coffee beans! From Rostov! From Rostov!
> You (I) have brought me (you) coffee beans!
> You (I) have brought me (you) beans!

(He waves the aroma at her. She nearly faints. They kiss. Then Ludmilla goes into the kitchen with the coffee. Meanwhile, Volodya has started home, across the stage.)

VOLODYA.
> Kolya. For three weeks.

(Happy to be home, Nikolai puts down his bags. He sees the wall calendar.)

NIKOLAI.
> A Stalin wall calendar.

(The page has not been changed. He is pleasantly perplexed.)
> February 9th?

(He starts to call for Ludmilla, just as Volodya is coming to the house. Together:)

VOLODYA and NIKOLAI.
> Ludmilla!

(Nikolai hears Volodya. Then the door starts to open. Nikolai playfully hides behind the door. Volodya enters. He sits and reads a paper. Nikolai jumps out. He puts his hands over Volodya's eyes. Volodya smiles. Thinking it is Ludmilla, he touches Nikolai's hands, tenderly. Then he starts kissing them. Ludmilla re-enters, carrying coffee and cups on a tray. She sees Volodya now kissing Nikolai on the mouth. Then — Ludmilla drops the tray, cups clattering. Volodya opens his eyes, sees Nikolai. Ludmilla and Volodya look at each other, terrified. But Nikolai just jumps away, laughing, thinking it has all been a big joke.)

NIKOLAI.
> I have brought you beans!

VOLODYA.
> Beans?

NIKOLAI.
> Coffee beans!

(With terrible relief, Ludmilla helps explain:)

LUDMILLA.
> Coffee beans!

LUDMILLA and NIKOLAI.
> From Rostov!
> From Rostov!

VOLODYA.   *(Not understanding.)*
> Coffee?

NIKOLAI.
> Beans! I have brought you coffee beans!

LUDMILLA and NIKOLAI.
> Coffee beans! From Rostov!

VOLODYA.   *(Understanding.)*
> You ... have ... brought ... me ... beans!

LUDMILLA.
> Beans!

NIKOLAI.
> Beans!

VOLODYA.
> Coffee beans!

ALL.
> Coffee beans!
> From Rostov! From Rostov!

LUDMILLA and VOLODYA.
> He has brought us coffee beans!

NIKOLAI.
> I have brought you ...

(With a dazed, relieved Volodya, a jubilant but strained dance of celebration begins. Ludmilla uses cups and spoons as little, desperate percussive accents.)

    Beans!

LUDMILLA and VOLODYA.
    He has brought us …

NIKOLAI.
    Beans!

(Nikolai pours beans into their hands, but they spill all over the floor. Spent, Ludmilla and Volodya scramble to pick them up. Lights fade. Lights up on the table. A little later that night. They finish dinner in silence. Volodya reads a book, distracted, his food untouched. Nikolai eats, indifferently, ravenously. Disturbed, watching them, Ludmilla takes their plates. Nikolai touches her hand with tenderness. Ludmilla discreetly pulls away. Then she takes the dishes into the kitchen. Nikolai watches her go, fondly. When she has gone, Volodya looks up from his book. As if he can stand it no longer, he turns to Nikolai. Nikolai is still looking fondly after Ludmilla. He turns to Volodya, to confide something, too. At once:)

VOLODYA and NIKOLAI.
    Well. Well.
    What? What?
    I …
    Nothing.

    I never speak in big and complicated ways.
    But this is big and complicated.
    It is not easy for me to say.

    I think the world of Ludmilla.
    She is so quiet and so dark.
    I hope that you will understand.
    Another man might not.
    But we have kissed each other many times
    And so we know each other well.
    Well, you and I.
    But, well, Ludmilla, also, and I
    Have kissed each other many times.
    That is what I meant.
    You see?

    I never speak in big and complicated ways.
    But love is big and complicated.
    I love Ludmilla.

(They look at each other.)
    What?

(Volodya gulps. Then, furiously:)

NIKOLAI.

    Not another word!

(Nikolai slams a fork down into the table, incensed. Then Ludmilla quickly brings in a steaming, smoking bowl of soup. Fuming, hurt, he tastes it. But it burns his mouth. He stands, suddenly, kicking away his chair. Ludmilla retreats back to the kitchen, afraid. Nikolai turns on Volodya. With great effort, he restrains his anger.)

    My friend, my friend.
    Do you mean to stay here?

(Volodya has gone back to his book. He keeps turning pages. No reply.)

    Do you mean to stay here?

(No reply.)

    Do you mean to stay here?

(Volodya slams his book shut. He explodes at him.)

VOLODYA.

    Yes!

(Pause. Then Nikolai nods.)

NIKOLAI.

    Then I shall go and you can live together.

(He exits, slamming the door behind him.)

    Then I shall go and you can live forever.

    Without my wife,
    I don't know where I'll go.
    Where will I go now?
    I'm not like other men.

    When I'm with my wife, I'm a man
    Whose flesh becomes a chest,
    Whose features make a face.

    My parts are put together
    When I'm with my wife.

    Without my wife,
    I'm falling like a flake of snow
    That slips into the mouths of people.
    Then gets swallowed up by people.
    I'm never good in snow.
    I wear a hood in snow.

    It's more than merely love.

    Without my wife,
    I don't know where I'll go.

>   Where will I go now?
>   I'm not like other men, I'll be lost.
>
>   I must get lodgings.
> *(Ludmilla comes back in, cautiously. She picks up the fallen chair. She looks at Volodya sitting there, alone. Then she sits beside him. They finish eating. Nikolai walks the streets outside. Ludmilla and Volodya go to the bed. Spoken:)*
>   There is a housing shortage!

ALL.
>   Short —
>   Shor —
>   Shh.
>   Stalin.
(Thunder and lighting. Nikolai puts his collar up and sings:)

NIKOLAI.
>   The world. Outside.
(Finally, Nikolai finds his "bed" at his work site, on the Bolshoi Opera roof. Ludmilla and Volodya go to the bed. They are kissing.)

LUDMILLA.
>   Inside. The home.

NIKOLAI.
>   The night. The cold. The rain.
(Ludmilla and Volodya try to remember the radio song.)

LUDMILLA and VOLODYA.
>   You send me over the, over the,
>   Over the moon!
>   Over the, over the ...
(Outside.)

NIKOLAI.
>   The night. The cold. The dark. The rain.

LUDMILLA and VOLODYA.
>   Over ...

NIKOLAI.
>   The moon.
(Volodya sits in the rocking chair. Ludmilla stays on the bed. Outside, Nikolai shivers, tries to sleep.)
>   It is so quiet and so dark.
>   I dream.
>   That I sit in my rocking chair.

>   Going back and forth and back and forth.
>   Ludmilla beside me.
>   The cat beside her.
>   I sit on the roof of the Bolshoi Opera
>   And dream.
>   The sky is a ceiling.

VOLODYA.
>   I sit in my rocking chair.
>   And dream.
>   That I march at a meeting.
>   Going back and forth and back and forth.
>   Ludmilla beside me.
>   The crowd behind her.
>   I sit in my rocking chair.
>   And dream.
>   The ceiling is a sky.

LUDMILLA.
>   I dream
>   It is noisy and bright.
>   I am wearing a hat
>   With a satin trim
>   And a flower on the brim.
>   A gift from him.
>   I am wearing a coat
>   With buttons made of bone
>   And a collar tightly sewn.
>   I am wearing a coat
>   That I bought on my own.
>   I never remember
>   My dreams.

(All three verses are sung at the same time. Then ... lights fade. Lights rise. Morning. Heavy wind outside. Ludmilla sits, contentedly, reading the paper. Then ... the door flies open. Nikolai stands there, miserable from the night. Ludmilla screams. Then ... she recovers. Nikolai squeezes his soaked scarf out onto the floor. He coughs, theatrically. Staring balefully at her, he goes offstage. Trying to ignore him, Ludmilla picks up her paper again. Nikolai re-enters, all bundled up. He tries to exit. The wind howls. He milks it, struggling to open the door. Then, finally, he manages to lurch out. No longer able to ignore Nikolai, Ludmilla throws her paper down and runs out, after him. The two of them return, Nikolai smiling, gratefully, a bit guilty. He dries her wet face, tenderly. She looks at him. She takes his belongings from his hand. Nikolai is terribly relieved. But then:)

>   I never speak in big and complicated ways.
>   But this is big and complicated.
>   It is not easy for me to say ...
>   We'll take the bed and you the sofa.

(Nikolai stares at her, crestfallen.)

NIKOLAI.
>I'll take the sofa and you the bed?

LUDMILLA.
>We'll take the bed and you the sofa.

NIKOLAI. *(It's sinking in.)*
>I'll take the sofa. I'll take the sofa.

LUDMILLA.
>You'll take the sofa, we'll take the bed.
>You'll take the sofa —

NIKOLAI.
>While you take the bed!
>The bed!

(He throws his hat and coat down, furiously.)
>You and I?

LUDMILLA.
>Bed and sofa.

(Behind them, Volodya enters from outside.)

NIKOLAI.
>You and he?

LUDMILLA.
>Sofa and bed.
>We and you —

NIKOLAI.
>Bed and sofa?

LUDMILLA.
>I and he —

NIKOLAI.
>Sofa and bed?

(Volodya helpfully pulls out the dressing screen.)

VOLODYA.
>The dressing screen.

NIKOLAI.
>Bed and sofa!

VOLODYA.
> You —

LUDMILLA.
> — and I —

NIKOLAI.
> — and I.

ALL.
> Sofa and Bed.
> You and I and I.
> Bed and sofa.
> You and I and I.
> Sofa and bed.
> You and I and I.
> And you.

NIKOLAI.
> So ... fantastic.

(They all stand there. Then Ludmilla and Volodya start to set up the new accommodations, positioning the screen. They check nervously to see if Nikolai approves. Lights fade.)

ANNOUNCER'S VOICE.
> In 1919, the bohemian "Imagist" school of poets
> published sensual works with such titles as
> "I Fornicate with Inspiration." The movement collapsed
> five years later.

(Lights up. Some nights later. Volodya and Nikolai play checkers. Ludmilla sits at the table with them. It is clear she and Volodya would very much like the game to end. Each yearns for the other.)

NIKOLAI.
> One, two, three ...

LUDMILLA and VOLODYA.
> A game of checkers!

VOLODYA.
> Ludmilla ...

LUDMILLA.
> ... Volodya ...

NIKOLAI.
> King me!

LUDMILLA.
> ... and his majesty. One, two, three.

VOLODYA.
> I dream. Ludmilla. The bed.

LUDMILLA.
> The bed. Volodya. I dream.

NIKOLAI.
> One, two, three ...

LUDMILLA.
> A game of checkers!

VOLODYA.
> Ludmilla ...

LUDMILLA.
> ... Volodya ...

NIKOLAI.
> King me!

LUDMILLA and VOLODYA.
> ... and Kolya.

(Whistling, Nikolai wins. Ludmilla and Volodya are glad it's over.)

NIKOLAI.
> Things may look black for me,
> but in the end, I always win!

VOLODYA. *(Rising, yawning.)*
> I'm tired.

(Nikolai sees this.)

LUDMILLA. *(Rising.)*
> The bed.

NIKOLAI. *(Starting to play again.)*

> One quick game!
> Red or black?

LUDMILLA. *(Sitting, sighing.)*
> Checkers!

VOLODYA. *(Sitting.)*
    Things look black.

NIKOLAI.
    I always win! Jump!

VOLODYA.
    One ...

NIKOLAI.
    Jump!

VOLODYA.
    Two!

NIKOLAI.
    Jump!

LUDMILLA and VOLODYA.
    Go back!
(Using checkers as eyeballs, Nikolai does a funny little dance, while sitting down.)

NIKOLAI.
    Things may look black for me,
    but in the end, I always win!
    Jump!

VOLODYA.
    Ludmilla.

NIKOLAI.
    Jump!

LUDMILLA.
    Volodya.

LUDMILLA and VOLODYA.
    We're tired.

VOLODYA.
    I dream. Ludmilla. The bed.

LUDMILLA.
    The bed. Volodya.

LUDMILLA and VOLODYA.
    I dream.

NIKOLAI.
>One, two, three ...
>A game of checkers.

VOLODYA.
>Ludmilla.

LUDMILLA.
>Volodya.

NIKOLAI.
>And Kolya.
>King me!

(Pointedly, Ludmilla rises. Starting to undress for bed, using the screen, she does a little striptease for Volodya. Volodya watches, fondly. Nikolai smacks him, makes Volodya turn away. Volodya peeks. Nikolai smacks him again. Then Volodya has an idea. To Nikolai:)

VOLODYA.
>I am hungry.

NIKOLAI. *(At the board.)*
>Shh!

VOLODYA.
>I am hungry now, Kolya.

NIKOLAI.
>You were tired.

VOLODYA.
>I am hungry now.

LUDMILLA and VOLODYA.
>Hungry! We are hungry now!
>Hungry! We are hungry *now!*

(Ludmilla and Volodya expect Nikolai to go out. But instead he starts towards the kitchen. Volodya stops him. Delicately:)

VOLODYA.
>You'll get the bread and I the soda.

NIKOLAI.
>You'll get the soda and I the bread?

VOLODYA.
>You and I.

35

NIKOLAI.
  Bread and soda?

VOLODYA.
  You and I.

NIKOLAI.
  Soda ... and bread.
(Nikolai reluctantly goes out. Volodya watches out the window and makes sure he is out of sight. Then, frantically unbuttoning his shirt, he runs to Ludmilla and the bed. They disappear behind the dressing screen. Lights shift. Nikolai returns, bread in hand. He hears the water bubbling, screaming. He runs offstage, to the kitchen, to turn it off. Then he returns. He notices clothes draped over the dressing screen.)
  The dressing screen.
(From behind the screen, sounds of lovemaking:)

VOLODYA'S VOICE.
  Ludmilla ...

LUDMILLA'S VOICE.
  ... Volodya ...

NIKOLAI.
  ... and Kolya.
(Dejected, Nikolai goes to the sofa. He tries to sleep. He counts sheep. As they moan:)
  One, two, three ...
(He puts a pillow over his ears, as lights fade. Lights up. Some nights later. Another checkers game. Now, both Volodya and Nikolai are engrossed in it, indifferent to Ludmilla. Frustrated, Ludmilla sits by the window.)

LUDMILLA.
  Every evening now.
  Checkers!
  Kolya, Volodya ...
  And Ludmilla.
  One, two, three.
(Ludmilla gives a little "hmph!" of frustration. Nikolai makes noises with his mouth, deciding how to move. Ludmilla sighs. She stands, tries a different tack. She puts on her shabby hat and coat. She goes to Volodya and starts teasing him, coquettishly.)
  Shall we go for a walk, Volodya?
  Shall we go for a walk?
  I am wearing a hat
  I bought when I was wed
  It's still a kind of red.
  I am wearing a hat
  That almost fits my head.
  Shall we go for a walk, Volodya?
  Shall we?

(Volodya looks up. Ludmilla is doing a sultry little dance, to entice him. Volodya rises, starts to join her. Then:)

NIKOLAI.
> King me!

(Volodya rushes back to the game. Stymied, Ludmilla just stares at him. Then:)

LUDMILLA.
> Shall we go for a walk, *(Turns.)* Kolya?
> Shall we go for a walk?
>
> I am wearing a coat
> At least a decade old
> But still a kind of gold.
> I am wearing a coat
> That always keeps me cold.
> Shall we go for a walk, Kolya?
> Shall we? Shall we? *Shall we?*

(Nikolai looks up. Ludmilla is doing a mad gypsy dance. He smiles. This time, she draws Nikolai up. Then:)

VOLODYA.
> King me!

(Nikolai scrambles back to the game, keeps playing. Incensed, Ludmilla turns on both of them.)

LUDMILLA.
> Do you mean to stay here?

(No reply.)
> Do you mean to stay here?

(No reply.)
> Do you mean to stay here?

(Nikolai and Volodya both look up now.)

VOLODYA and NIKOLAI.
> Yes!

(There is a beat. Then:)

LUDMILLA.
> Then I shall go and you can live together.

(Haughtily, Ludmilla starts for the door. But with her hand on the knob, she sighs, beaten. She goes back to sit by the window. Volodya and Nikolai go back to their game. She gives another little "hmph!" of frustration. Lights fade. Lights rise. Another night. Ludmilla sits on the bed, staring off. Volodya listens to his radio with his headphones. Then he takes off the headset.)

VOLODYA.
> Ludmilla.

(She looks up, expectantly.)
>I am hungry.
>I am hungry now.

(She just looks at him.)

LUDMILLA.
>Hungry? I'm tired.

VOLODYA.
>I am hungry. Now —
>You'll get the bread and you'll get the soda.

(Ludmilla stares at him. Then she rises, starts throwing on her hat and coat.)

LUDMILLA.
>I'll get the soda? I'll get the bread?

(Volodya angrily rises.)

VOLODYA.
>You are more fond of Kolya than of me!

LUDMILLA.
>Loud as the other!
>And just as bad!

(Ludmilla defiantly goes out of the apartment. Volodya runs after her. Outside:)

VOLODYA.
>You will not leave!
>I am your husband!

LUDMILLA.
>I seldom have the honor.

VOLODYA.
>You are more fond of Kolya than of me!

LUDMILLA.
>Blonde hair. And a sensitive face.

VOLODYA.
>I am your husband!

LUDMILLA.
>Your majesty.

VOLODYA.
>You'll get the bread and you'll get soda!

LUDMILLA.
>   Inside. Outside. I get.

VOLODYA.
>   I am your husband.
>   You will not leave.

LUDMILLA.
>   Loud as the other. And just as bad.

VOLODYA.
>   And don't forget to scrub —

LUDMILLA.
>   The home? The world?

VOLODYA.
>   — the floor!

(Volodya exits.)

BLACKOUT

Lights rise on the apartment. Ludmilla stands near the table. She pours herself a glass of vodka.

ANNOUNCER'S VOICE.
>   In Russia, it is a commonly held belief that
>   drinking vodka stretches the vocal cords.

(She downs it. Then she slugs from the bottle itself. She shudders, broadly. Then she places a glass opposite her, as if for a friend.)

LUDMILLA.
>   The Soviet Union is my sister.
>   She is my twin.
>
>   We should have a drink
>   And talk about our men.
>   Maybe more than one drink.
>   My sister would say that she and I
>   Go back and forth and back and forth
>   From one tyrant to another.
>   We make revolutions that go round
>   In circles that grow smaller.
>   Till they're very small.

> I'd tell my twin that
> Maybe on the next turn
> You won't trust your leaders,
> I won't trust my lovers.
> When we turn to them,
> They turn on us.
> When will we learn not to turn?
>
> Then we'd drink so much
> We'd both be still.
>
> Here's to our men,
> Be they peasant or Czar.
> They're all just the same
> In the USSR.

(*Now drunk, Ludmilla clinks the two glasses in a toast. Then she heads for the bed. She takes one step, stops, stunned, and falls on her face. After a moment, she crawls over to the bed and scales her way up onto it. Sitting there, she groggily combs her hair with her fingers. Volodya enters. He sees the half-empty bottle on the table and snorts, contemptuously. He approaches the bed. Ludmilla looks at him. Then she tosses a pillow at him. He is shocked.*)

> I'll take the bed, you — the sofa.

VOLODYA.
> I'll take the sofa and you — you — the bed?
> You and I?

LUDMILLA. (*Nods.*)
> Bed. Sofa.

VOLODYA.
> I and you?

LUDMILLA.
> So unhappy.

(*They go to their separate posts. They try to sleep. Lights shift. We hear rustling at the door. Nikolai is trying it, but it is locked. Then, in the dim, Nikolai comes through the window. He is a little drunk. He sees the sleeping arrangements and laughs to himself. He sits in the rocking chair between the two, contented. Ludmilla lifts her head, sees him. She goes to Nikolai, kneels near his chair, tenderly. She strokes his hair. He is very pleased.*)

NIKOLAI.
> It is so quiet and so dark.
> I sit in my rocking chair.
> Going back and forth and back and forth.
> Ludmilla beside me.
> Volodya beside me.

(*She rises, goes back to the bed. She looks at him, waiting for him to follow. Just as he starts to, Volodya stirs. Nikolai stops. He settles back into his chair. Ludmilla has returned to the bed. Volodya sleeps on the sofa.*)

    I sit in my rocking chair.
    And dream.
(*Lights fade.*)

ANNOUNCER'S VOICE.
    Tolstoy wrote that "uniting with the object
    of one's love is an aim unworthy of human beings."
    But, unfortunately, there are none of his books in this apartment.
(*Lights up. Ludmilla is scrubbing clothes in a basin. Volodya is on the couch, reading and rustling a newspaper. Nikolai is at the table, doing construction figuring, tapping a pencil on a water pitcher. They establish a rhythmic pattern. Then ... Ludmilla seems to falter. Neither man notices. Ludmilla recovers. They go back to work: scrubbing, rustling, tapping. Then Ludmilla falters again. This time, Volodya notices.*)

VOLODYA.
    What's the matter?

NIKOLAI.
    Women.
(*They go back to work: scrubbing, rustling, tapping. Then Ludmilla falters once more. This time, Volodya approaches.*)

VOLODYA.
    What's the matter?

NIKOLAI.
    Crazy.
(*Ludmilla tries to go back to work, but she cannot.*)

VOLODYA.
    What's the matter?

NIKOLAI.
    Nothing.

VOLODYA.
    Shall we have some soda?
    Shall we have some coffee?
    Shall we go for a walk, Ludmilla?
    Shall we go for a walk?

LUDMILLA.
    No.
(*Volodya gives her a sip of water.*)

VOLODYA.
  Is it better?

LUDMILLA.
  Oh, yes.

NIKOLAI.
  Nothing.
(Volodya gives her another sip.)

VOLODYA.
  Is it better?

LUDMILLA.
  Thank you.

NIKOLAI.
  Crazy.
(Volodya gives her another sip. She finishes off the glass.)

VOLODYA.
  Is it better?

NIKOLAI.
  Women.
(Volodya goes back to his newspaper. Then ... she falters once more. This time, she cannot rise so easily. Then:)

LUDMILLA.
  I am going
  To have a child.
(Volodya looks up.)

VOLODYA.
  To have a child.
(Nikolai looks up, too, from his desk.)

NIKOLAI.
  To have a child.

VOLODYA and NIKOLAI.
  She is going
  To have a child.
  A child!
(Nikolai looks at the wall, at the calendar. He counts.)

NIKOLAI.
  A Stalin wall calendar.
  One, two, three.

(The two men look at each other. Ludmilla watches them.)

LUDMILLA.
>I am going
>To have a child.

VOLODYA.
>To have my child.

NIKOLAI.
>To have someone else's child.

VOLODYA.
>The pride. The family. The name.

NIKOLAI.
>The shame. The gossip. The pain.

LUDMILLA.
>I am going
>To have someone else's child.

(The two men confront each other.)

NIKOLAI.
>You took the bed, I the sofa!

VOLODYA.
>I took the sofa and you the bed!

VOLODYA and NIKOLAI.
>You or I?
>Bed or sofa?
>You or I?
>Sofa or bed?
>Bed! Bed! Bed!

(They stop. Then they turn to Ludmilla.)

NIKOLAI.
>You are not going
>To have a child!

VOLODYA.
>To have my child!

NIKOLAI.
>No child of his —

VOLODYA.
>A child of mine —

NIKOLAI.
>Will ever be born.
>As long as I live.

VOLODYA.
>A wife of his —

NIKOLAI.
>No wife of mine —

VOLODYA.
>She would always be torn.

NIKOLAI.
>It's what she must give.

VOLODYA.
>You have to go —

NIKOLAI.
>— to the hospital.

VOLODYA.
>You have to have —

NIKOLAI.
>— an abortion.

VOLODYA and NIKOLAI.
>You are not going
>To have a child!

(Slowly then, Ludmilla starts for the window.)

LUDMILLA.
>I am someone
>Who is not going
>To have a child.

(They watch her, not moving.)

VOLODYA.
>What's the matter?

LUDMILLA.
>Nothing.

(Ludmilla reaches the window, sits by it. Then, slowly, the two men go back to work, rustling and tapping. Then, looking up:)

NIKOLAI.
>Women.

(Lights slowly fade. When lights rise, Ludmilla is in the "outside" area. It is a small hospital waiting room. There are other women, but they are not visible. In her lap, Ludmilla holds a number on a piece of paper. A dressing screen is visible. From behind it, a dress is thrown, as if being removed. Ludmilla waits, in silence. Then:)

LUDMILLA.
>I am alone.
>With other women.
>Women who sit.
>Women who knit.
>Women who stay all day.
>Going back and forth and back and forth.
>Inside the waiting room.
>Beside the dressing screen.
>The stain. The drain.

(Then ... a Doctor's Voice is heard:)

DOCTOR'S VOICE.
>One!

LUDMILLA.
>One leaves.

DOCTOR'S VOICE.
>One!

LUDMILLA.
>One leaves.

DOCTOR'S VOICE.
>One!

LUDMILLA.
>One leaves.

(Another dress comes over the dressing screen.)
>I am alone.
>With other women.
>Women who weep.
>Women who worry.
>Who say they'll stay.
>Going back and forth and back and forth.
>Inside the waiting room.
>Beside the dressing screen.
>The stain. The drain.

(Then:)

DOCTOR'S VOICE.
>Two!

LUDMILLA.
>Two leaves.

DOCTOR'S VOICE.
>Two!

LUDMILLA.
>Two leaves.

DOCTOR'S VOICE.
>Two!

LUDMILLA.
>Two leaves.
(Another dress comes over. Then — the air feels close to Ludmilla. She rises. She opens the window. She looks out. Suddenly, we hear ... a baby cry. Then ... looking out:)
>Outside the window.
>A baby.

>A baby in a blanket in a basket.
>With a Stalin doll.
>Outside the window.
>Someone else's child.
(She keeps watching. Then ... suddenly:)

DOCTOR'S VOICE.
>Three!

LUDMILLA.
>Three leaves.

DOCTOR'S VOICE.
>Three!

LUDMILLA.
>Three leaves.

DOCTOR'S VOICE.
>Three!

LUDMILLA.
>Three leaves.

(Another dress comes over. Then ... a woman's scream is heard. With more urgency — circling her seat:)
>Alone.
>With other women.
>Women who panic.
>Women who faint.
>Who say they'll pray.
>Going back and forth and back and forth.
>Inside — waiting.
>Inside — screaming.
>The stain. The drain.

(Ludmilla looks out the window again. More urgency:)
>Outside the window.
>A baby.
>
>In a blanket in a basket.
>With a Stalin, with a Stalin doll.
>Outside the window.
>Someone else's child.

(Then:)

DOCTOR'S VOICE.
>Four!

(Silence, then:)
>Four! Four!

(Then ... still looking out the window:)

LUDMILLA.
>I am not ...
>Four!

(Ludmilla runs out then, leaving her number on her chair. Beat. Then Volodya and Nikolai enter, from the opposite direction. They are better dressed. Their hair is combed. Each carries a bouquet of flowers.)

VOLODYA and NIKOLAI.
>We are her husband!
>Ludmilla's husband!
>We bathed and we shaved
>And we brought her flowers.
>We are her husband!

(Beat. Then ... they see no one is there. We still hear:)

DOCTOR'S VOICE.
>Four!

(Slowly, Volodya and Nikolai pick up the number Ludmilla has dropped. Lights fade. In the apartment, Ludmilla looks around at everything. Then she starts for the wall.)

LUDMILLA.
>The photograph of my face in a frame.

(She removes the photograph from its frame, takes it to the table, then writes on its back.)
>... away ...
>... believe ...
>... you ...
>... worthy ...

(She looks at it, rereading.)
>... I ...
>... do ...
>... either ...
>... To be ...
>... Goodbye ...

(Ludmilla puts down the photo. Then she rises and picks up bags that have already been packed. She puts on her coat and hat.)
>I am wearing a coat.
>I am wearing a hat.

(She takes a last look around.)
>I seldom have the honor
>Of going out.

(Then Ludmilla exits. Within seconds of her leaving, Volodya and Nikolai return home. They enter. They stop. They see the letter Ludmilla has written on the table. Nikolai picks it up and reads it.)

NIKOLAI.
>"I am going away.
>I do not believe
>That either of you
>is worthy to be ...
>A father.
>Goodbye. Ludmilla."

(He hands it to Volodya. He reads.)

VOLODYA.
>"I am going away.
>I do not believe
>That either of you
>is ..."

VOLODYA and NIKOLAI.
>"... worthy to be a father."

(They repeat it. Walking outside, Ludmilla sings the letter also. Until:)

ALL.
>"... worthy to be a father."

NIKOLAI.
>Our child.

VOLODYA and NIKOLAI.
Goodbye. *(They call for her.)* Ludmilla!
(They put the paper down, with great sadness. Then — resigned — regrouping:)

NIKOLAI.
I'll take the bed and you the sofa?

VOLODYA.
You'll take the sofa and I the bed?

VOLODYA and NIKOLAI.
You and I.
Bed and sofa.
You and I.
Sofa and bed.
(Outside, Ludmilla is approaching the "travel" area from which Volodya arrived.)

LUDMILLA.
Outside! The world!
1927. Moscow. Russia.
(Inside — the men start to settle in.)

VOLODYA and NIKOLAI.
The world. Inside.

LUDMILLA.
The train! The train! The train!
The birds! The morning! The sun!
The bridge! The city! The sky!

NIKOLAI.
The brush. The water. The wash.

VOLODYA.
The dressing screen.

NIKOLAI.
The cat. The tea.

VOLODYA and NIKOLAI.
The table. With two leaves.

VOLODYA.
Inside, it is quiet and dark.

NIKOLAI.
The stain.

VOLODYA.
> The drain.

VOLODYA and NIKOLAI.
> 13 Meschanskaia Lane.

(At the same time:)

LUDMILLA.
> The train! The train! The train!

NIKOLAI.
> The brush. The water. The wash.

VOLODYA.
> The cat. The tea. The table.

LUDMILLA.
> The birds! The morning! The sun!

NIKOLAI.
> The dressing screen.

LUDMILLA.
> The bridge! The country!
> The country! The sky!
> The sky! The sky!
> Outside, it is noisy and bright.

NIKOLAI.
> The world. Inside.

LUDMILLA.
> Outside! The world!

VOLODYA and NIKOLAI.   *(Spoken.)*
> Jump! Jump! Jump!

LUDMILLA.   *(Sung.)*
> The future! The world!

ALL.
> 1927. Moscow. Russia.

(Outside, Ludmilla gets on the train. Inside, Volodya and Nikolai take their respective sleeping areas.)

VOLODYA and NIKOLAI.
> The bed. The sofa.

LUDMILLA.
    The sky!
(Then:)

VOLODYA and NIKOLAI.
    I dream. Ludmilla. I dream.

LUDMILLA.
    He will have blonde hair and a sensitive face.

VOLODYA and NIKOLAI.
    I never speak in big and complicated ways.
    But love is big and complicated.
(Beat. Then:)

ALL.
    Not another word.

VOLODYA.
    Shh.

NIKOLAI.
    Shh.

LUDMILLA.
    Shh.
(Ludmilla travels. She waves goodbye to her home. Volodya and Nikolai lie awake. For a while. In silence. Then ... lights slowly fade.)

THE END

PROPERTY LIST

Bag (VOLODYA)
Calendar with daily pages to tear (NIKOLAI)
Plate of runny cooked eggs (LUDMILLA)
Dust cloth (LUDMILLA)
Radio (LUDMILLA, VOLODYA)
Sandwich (NIKOLAI)
Official paper (VOLODYA)
Newspaper in wrapped bundle (VOLODYA)
Telegram (NIKOLAI)
Packed bag (LUDMILLA)
Pack of cards (NIKOLAI)
Small box of coffee beans (NIKOLAI)
Tray with spoons and coffee cups with coffee (LUDMILLA)
Book (VOLODYA)
Fork (NIKOLAI)
Bowl of hot soup (LUDMILLA)
Checkers game board and pieces (NIKOLAI, VOLODYA)
Bread (NIKOLAI)
Newspaper (LUDMILLA)
Headphones (VOLODYA)
Vodka bottle (LUDMILLA)
Drinking glasses (LUDMILLA)
Pillow (VOLODYA, LUDMILLA)
Basin (LUDMILLA)
Clothes (LUDMILLA)
Pencil (NIKOLAI, LUDMILLA)
Water pitcher (NIKOLAI)
Glass of water (VOLODYA)
Piece of paper with numbers (LUDMILLA)
Dresses
Photograph in frame (LUDMILLA)

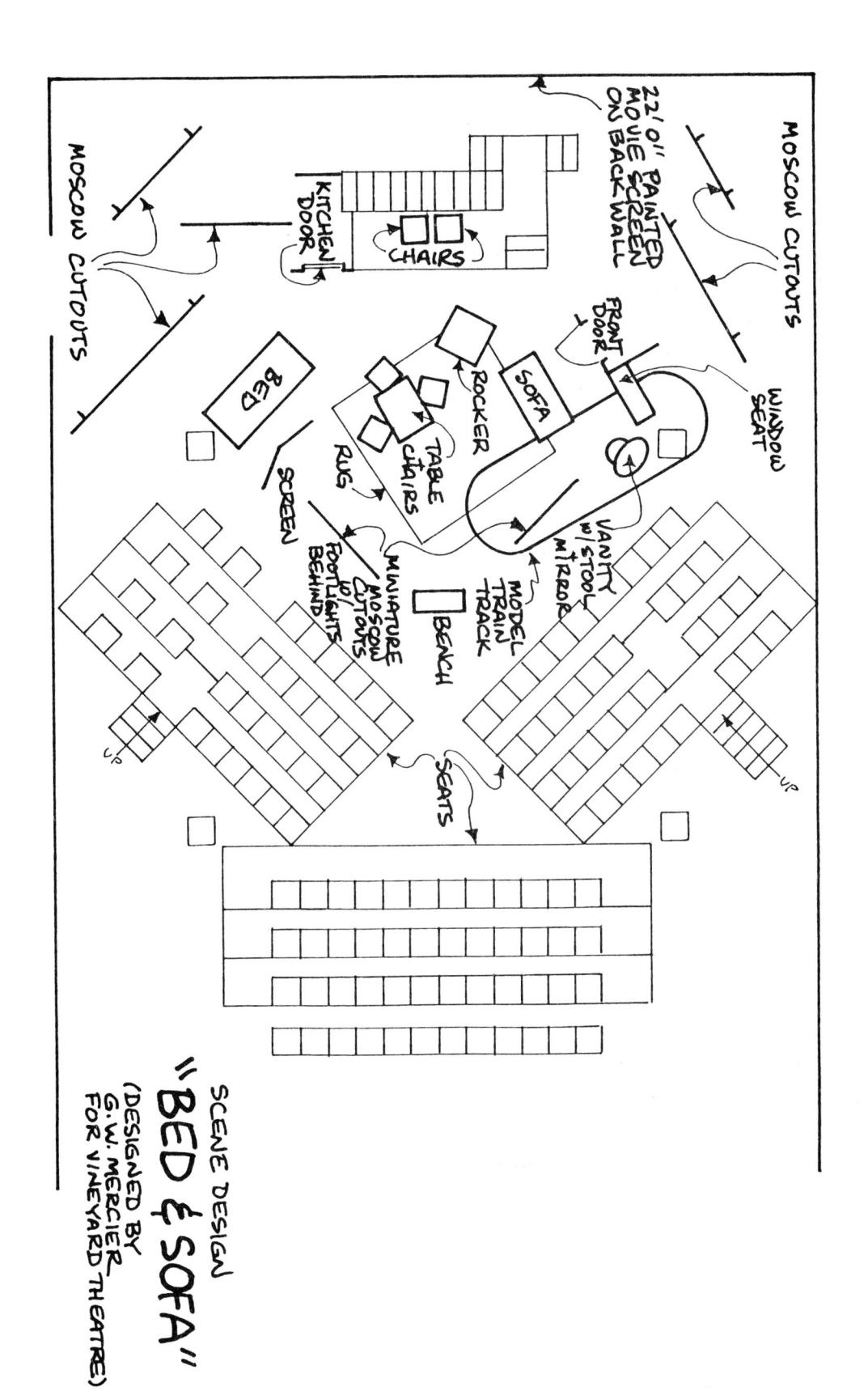

SCENE DESIGN
"BED & SOFA"
(DESIGNED BY G.W. MERCIER FOR VINEYARD THEATRE)